The Nature Company
Young Discoveries Library

Underwater Animals

Written by Helen Cooney

TIME
LIFE
BOOKS

**The Nature Company Young Discoveries Library
is published by Time-Life Books.**

Conceived and produced by
Weldon Owen Pty Limited
43 Victoria Street, McMahons Point,
NSW, 2060, Australia
A member of the
Weldon Owen Group of Companies
Sydney • San Francisco

THE NATURE COMPANY
Priscilla Wrubel, Ed Strobin, Steve Manning,
Georganne Papac, Tracy Fortini

TIME-LIFE BOOKS
Time-Life Books is a division of Time Life Inc.
Time-Life is a trademark of Time Warner Inc. U.S.A.

Vice President and Publisher: Terry Newell
Editorial Director: Donia A. Steele
Director of New Product Development: Regina Hall
Director of Sales: Neil Levin
Director of Financial Operations: J. Brian Birky

WELDON OWEN Pty Limited
President: John Owen
Publisher: Sheena Coupe
Managing Editor: Rosemary McDonald
Project Editor: Jenni Bruce
Text Editor: Claire Craig
Art Director: Sue Burk
Designer: Liz Seymour
Picture Research: Libby Frederico
Production Manager: Caroline Webber
Vice President, International Sales: Stuart Laurence
Coeditions Director: Derek Barton
Subject Consultants: Dr. David Kirshner,
Terence Lindsey, Dr. George McKay, Craig Sowden

Library of Congress
Cataloging-in-Publication Data
Underwater animals / Helen Cooney.
    p. cm. -- (Young discoveries)

  ISBN 0-7835-4841-9

  1. Marine animals--Juvenile literature.
[1. Marine animals.] I. Title. II. Series.
QL122.2.C656   1996
591.92--dc20   96-16966

Manufactured by Mandarin Offset
Printed in China

A Weldon Owen Production

Contents

Some whales eat more than a truckload of tiny shrimp every day!

▶ Many ocean animals are swift swimmers. Sea lions flap their flippers, whales beat their tails, and fish wave their fins. Squid swim by spurting jets of water out through their bodies.

— UNDERWATER ANIMALS —

A Watery World

Many of the world's most marvelous creatures spend their lives in water. In freshwater ponds and rivers, and in salty bays and seas, creatures of every size, shape, and color search for food. In the ocean, big animals, such as the black and white orca, eat smaller ones, such as sea lions. Sea lions eat salmon and squid. A torpedo-shaped squid can speed through the water to catch herring with the suckers on its long tentacles.

4

▼ Salmon feed on schools
of herring. Herring eat
tiny plants and animals,
called plankton, which
they filter from the water.

5

▲ Parrotfish change more than their colors as they grow. Some start out as black and yellow babies, become brown females, and end up as colorful males!

▶ Sharks are the largest fish in the sea. Whale sharks swallow tiny floating plants and animals, while white sharks rip flesh with their razor-sharp teeth.

— U N D E R W A T E R A N I M A L S —

Fish Big and Small

Fish come in thousands of shapes, colors, and sizes. Some are see-through. Others are completely black. The tiniest fish, the dwarf goby, is smaller than your thumbnail. The largest is the whale shark, which can be nearly eight times the length of a person! All fish live in salty or fresh water. They breathe underwater using gills and have fins for swimming. Most fish have skeletons made from bone, but sharks and rays have skeletons made from a tough, elastic tissue called cartilage.

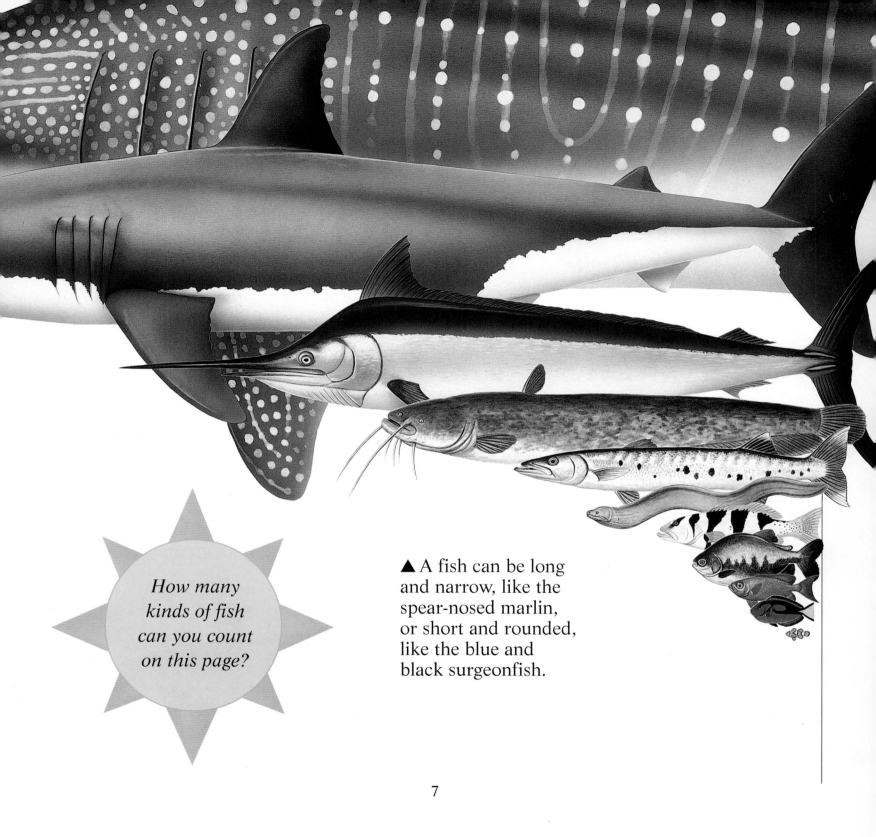

How many kinds of fish can you count on this page?

▲ A fish can be long and narrow, like the spear-nosed marlin, or short and rounded, like the blue and black surgeonfish.

Shark Showdown

▲ The zebra shark has stripes when it is a baby. These stripes change to spots as it grows. Zebra sharks like to eat slimy sea snails and hard crabs.

Many people think that sharks are the most dangerous creatures in the sea. But not all sharks have huge, crushing jaws and jagged teeth. The largest shark of all, the whale shark, has tiny teeth. It strains shrimp from the water through its gills. Many smaller sharks nestle in sand on the sea floor where they crunch through crabs and shellfish with their tough teeth. Other sharks must swim all the time to keep water flowing across their gills. If they stop, they will sink to the bottom and drown.

▶ The leopard shark has many spots. It searches for crabs in shallow, muddy water.

▼ Like all sharks, the white shark replaces its teeth. It always has a row of new teeth growing behind its front teeth.

The tiny cookiecutter shark chews neat holes in a whale's flesh.

Pointy snouts help sharks swim fast

Open Wide!

Eels are long, slim, snakelike fish. The eels in tropical waters have spots and stripes so they can hide among the swaying coral branches. The gulper is the strangest eel in the sea. It lives in the cold, dark ocean depths, where food is scarce. With huge, elastic jaws that open like an umbrella, it gulps down anything that swims its way.

◀ This deep-sea hatchetfish is about to become the gulper eel's meal. The gulper's mouth has a fringe of tiny, prickly teeth.

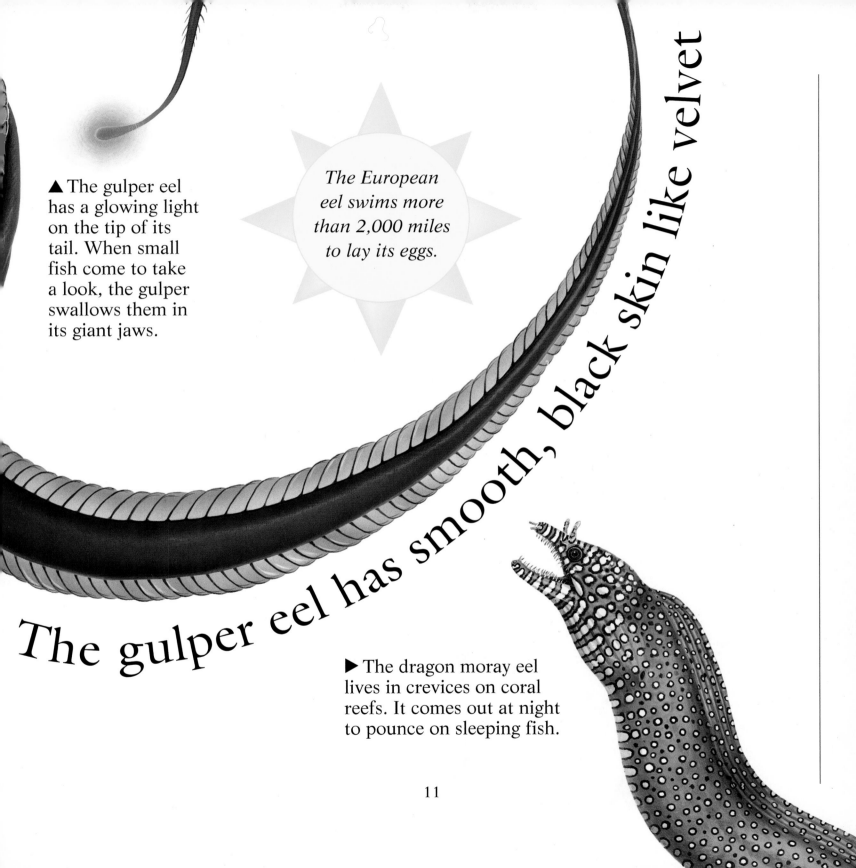

▲ The gulper eel has a glowing light on the tip of its tail. When small fish come to take a look, the gulper swallows them in its giant jaws.

The European eel swims more than 2,000 miles to lay its eggs.

The gulper eel has smooth, black skin like velvet

▶ The dragon moray eel lives in crevices on coral reefs. It comes out at night to pounce on sleeping fish.

11

Horses of the Sea

Most sea horses can change their color to disguise themselves from enemies.

There are plenty of fish in the sea, but none is quite like the sea horse. It swims with its head up and tail down, and looks like a tiny pony bobbing in the water. Sea horses and their cousins, the pipefish, have long, thin bodies covered by a bony armor. They all suck up small sea creatures through their long snouts. The sea horse curls its monkeylike tail around waving seaweed and coral stems while it waits for food to pass by.

▲ Head or tail? The zebra pipefish's yellow tail spot makes its tail look like a head. The black eye stripe makes its head look like a tail.

12

▶ Male sea horses, like this one, give birth to babies. The female sea horse lays her eggs inside a pouch on the father's belly. Here the babies grow into miniature sea horses.

Hard Cases

◀ Some spiny lobsters link up before marching across the ocean floor. There can be as many as 60 lobsters in a line. The lobster behind always touches the one in front.

Crabs and lobsters are creatures called crustaceans. Instead of bones, crustaceans have a hard shell that completely covers their soft insides and protects them from pecking birds and hungry fish. Crustaceans live in all sorts of places, from freshwater lakes to salty seas. Some crabs scuttle about in shallow tide pools searching for scraps of food. Others live in burrows in the sandy shore. Lobsters crawl about the ocean floor. They can make a sudden dash from danger with a flick of their powerful tail.

Crabs and lobsters breathe through feathery gills inside their hard shells.

14

◄ The hermit crab makes its home in old sea-snail shells. When the shell gets too tight, it moves into something roomier.

Crabs' eyes are raised on stalks

▼ Crabs use their large front claws, called pincers, to grip and rip food.

Slippery Swimmers

Frogs and salamanders are amphibians. Most amphibians start life as tiny, wiggly tadpoles in freshwater ponds or streams. They breathe through gills and swim with flattened tails. As they grow, the tadpoles get ready for life on land. They sprout four legs and use lungs inside their bodies to breathe. Most frogs and salamanders do not stray far from water. They must keep their moist, slimy skin from drying out.

▶ Splash! Many frogs have webbed toes to help them push through the water.

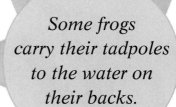

Some frogs carry their tadpoles to the water on their backs.

▼ The mudpuppy is a salamander. Unlike most other amphibians, it spends its whole life in the water. It breathes through frilly red gills.

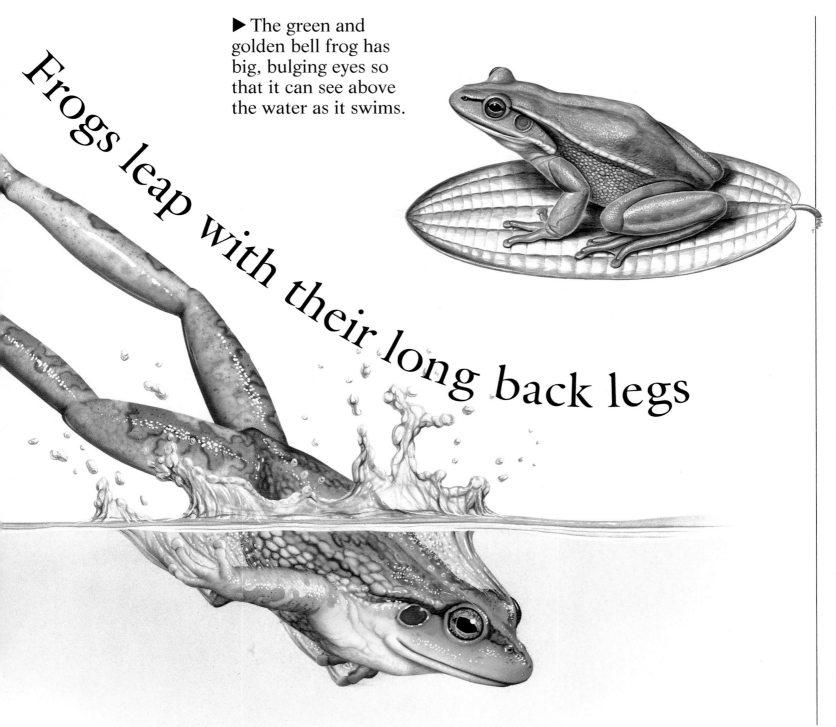

► The green and golden bell frog has big, bulging eyes so that it can see above the water as it swims.

Frogs leap with their long back legs

Water Lizards

Lots of lizards live near water. Some search for insects among riverside plants. Others will leap into streams to escape their enemies. The marine iguana from the Galápagos Islands is the only lizard that spends most of its time in the sea. It dives under the waves to munch on plants called algae, which grow on rocks. When it comes out of the cold water, it clings to the slippery rocks with its strong claws and warms up in the hot sun.

Marine iguanas swallow seawater and sneeze the salt out through their nostrils.

18

◀ Marine iguanas have black skin to help them soak up warmth from the sun. The males turn red and green at breeding time when they are trying to attract a mate.

▲ The basilisk lizard darts across the surface of the water on its back legs. It has special scaly fringes on its back toes to stop it from sinking.

Tranquil Turtles

▲ The painted turtle
clings to pond rocks
with its strong claws
and swims with its
webbed toes.

A turtle's shell gives it great protection. Most
turtles can pull their head, legs, and tail
inside their shell if enemies threaten them.
Some turtles live both on land and in water.
Pond turtles paddle through water with
webbed toes and bask on riverbanks
to keep warm. Sea turtles swim in
the ocean with broad, flat flippers.
They sometimes venture onto land
to lay their eggs in soft sand.

◀ The softshell turtle
breathes through its
narrow snout, which
pokes out of the water
like a snorkel.

20

Gliding silently through the sea

▼ The largest turtle in the sea is the leatherback turtle. Instead of a hard, bony shell, it has tough, leathery skin. Most of the time, it swims at a slow and steady pace, looking for jellyfish and other food.

Turtles are toothless. They snip off pieces of food with the hard plates covering their jaws.

Snappy Swimmers

Crocodiles and alligators spend most of their time lazing on the riverbank in the sun or floating very still in the water. When an animal such as a deer or a raccoon comes to the river for a drink, a crocodile may launch a surprise attack. It rockets out of the water with lightning speed and snaps with its powerful jaws and strong teeth. Crocodiles and alligators are fierce hunters but gentle parents. A mother will carefully pick up her newly hatched young in her mouth to carry them to water.

▲ Is it an alligator or a crocodile? When its mouth is closed, you can only see an alligator's top teeth.

▲ When a crocodile's mouth is closed, you can see its top teeth and some of its bottom teeth.

▼ Some alligators can survive for a short time in the chilly water beneath frozen ponds. They poke their nostrils out of small holes to breathe.

22

▲ With only eyes, ears, and noses showing above the water, crocodiles stay well hidden as they swim toward their prey.

Crocodiles and alligators can go for months without eating.

23

Feathered Friends

Some penguins stay underwater for 18 minutes without taking a breath.

Many birds spend a lot of time in and around water, searching for food. Most water birds have sleek, waterproof feathers to keep them warm and dry, and webbed feet for paddling. Ducks, geese, and swans nibble on water plants in ponds. Pelicans bob beneath the water's surface to catch fish in their enormous bills. Penguins cannot fly through the air, but they can swim underwater by flapping their stiff flippers. They spend most of the day chasing fish in the sea.

◀ Most penguins waddle when they come ashore, but the rockhopper penguin jumps along with its feet together.

24

A pelican's pouch is made of skin

▲ The brown pelican uses its beak like a fishing net to scoop up small fish swimming near the surface. To reach fish deeper down, it will dive headfirst into the sea.

25

Furry Swimmers

▲ Raccoons wade in water while they look for food. They always wash their meal before eating it.

Beavers, otters, and raccoons live in or near the water. Some of these furry swimmers have webbed feet and most have special hair to keep them warm and dry. Sea otters eat, sleep, and have their babies on the water's surface. Beavers chew through trees with their gigantic front teeth. They eat the leaves and bark, and use the branches to build special homes in the water, called lodges. Raccoons venture out after dark to find frogs and fish in streams and pools.

Beavers can chomp through a tree trunk in about ten minutes!

▶The sea otter cracks open spiny sea urchins by smashing them against a rock balanced on its chest.

A beaver's home is called a lodge

▼ This picture lets you see inside the beavers' lodge. The entrance is underwater to keep out land-dwelling enemies. The beavers leave a hole in the roof to let in fresh air.

◄ Sea lions lie in the sun to stay warm.

Salty Sea Lions

Sea lions are sea mammals, like seals and walruses. Although they spend much of their time in the ocean, they come back to shore to have their babies, which are called pups. Sea lions swim by sweeping their wide front flippers through the water. On land, they waddle over rocks with their back flippers bent forward. Hundreds of sea lions gather on rocky coasts in large, noisy groups called colonies. They bark, grunt, and bellow to each other.

28

▼ Sea lions have big, round eyes and sensitive whiskers to search for octopus, squid, and fish in underwater seaweed forests.

How many sea lions can you see searching for food?

Whales and Dolphins

Whales and dolphins spend their whole life in water. Under their skin they have a thick layer of fat, called blubber, to keep them warm. Like all mammals, they breathe with lungs, so they must swim to the surface to take breaths through nostrils on the top of their heads. Some whales have teeth and eat fish, squid, or even seals. Others strain tiny sea creatures from the water through bristly plates, called baleen, in their jaws.

The blue whale is the world's largest animal. It weighs more than 2,300 people.

▼ Dolphins are actually small whales. These fast swimmers sometimes jump out of the water, twisting and somersaulting in the air.

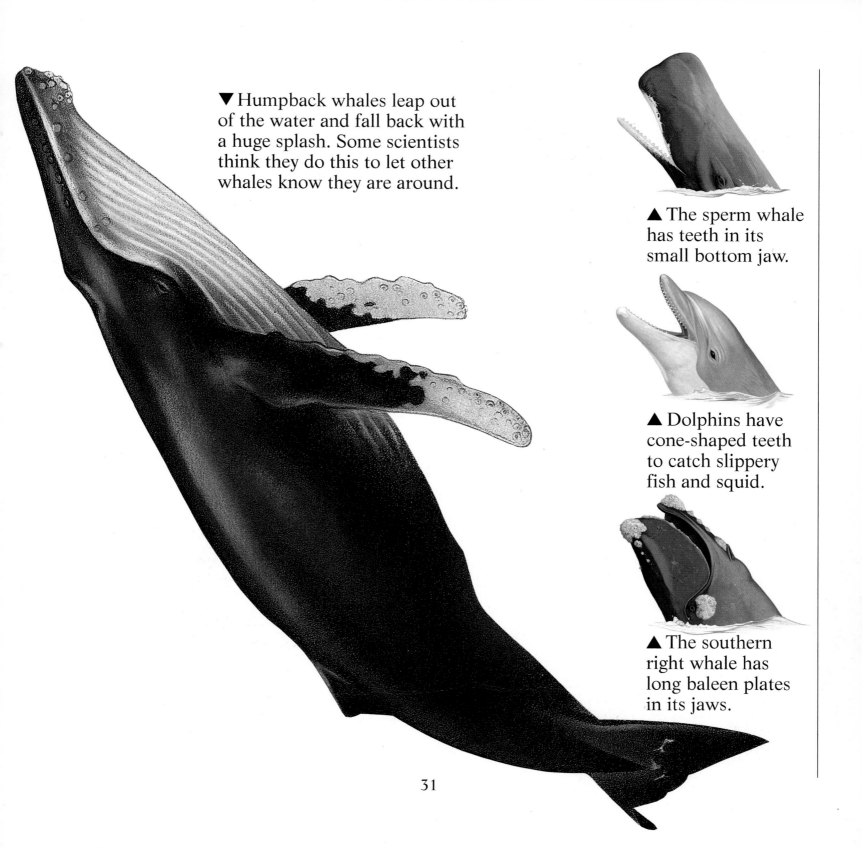

▼ Humpback whales leap out of the water and fall back with a huge splash. Some scientists think they do this to let other whales know they are around.

▲ The sperm whale has teeth in its small bottom jaw.

▲ Dolphins have cone-shaped teeth to catch slippery fish and squid.

▲ The southern right whale has long baleen plates in its jaws.

31

Other titles in the series:

Acknowledgments

(t=top, b=bottom, l=left, r=right, c=center, F=front cover, B=back cover)

Graham Back, 12bl, 13r. **André Boos,** 26tl, 27tr.
Martin Camm, 31r. **Simone End,** Fb, 20/21c, 22bl, 28tl, 28/29c.
Christer Eriksson, 1, 9c, 15tl, 15b. **Robert Hynes,** 18/19c.
David Kirshner, Ftr, B, 2, 3bl, 3tr, 5br, 6l, 6/7t, 8b, 10/11c, 11br, 12c, 13l, 16bl, 17tr, 19tr, 20tl, 20bl, 22tl, 22/23t, 24bl, 32.
James McKinnon, 26/27bc. **Tony Pyrzakowski,** 8tl, 30b, 31c.
Trevor Ruth, 14l. **Rod Scott,** 4cl, 4/5c, 5bl. **Kevin Stead,** 16/17c, 25c.